Disney · PIXAR

The COLOR of PIXAR

By TIA KRATTER   Foreword By JOHN LASSETER

CHRONICLE BOOKS
SAN FRANCISCO

FOREWORD

We always strive to make our films beautiful and to make you want to be in the worlds we've created. One of the most important tools we have as filmmakers is color. Color doesn't just make things beautiful; it makes things emotional. Color helps bring viewers into the moment with our characters, helps them feel what the characters are feeling. So it's essential that the color of a scene always be true to its emotion.

The frames you'll see in this book were created to be seen in the blink of an eye, each one appearing onscreen for just 1/24 of a second at a time. But each one is a work of art in itself, representing the contributions of many talented artists. I hope you'll enjoy their heartfelt feeling as much as their gorgeous color.

JOHN LASSETER

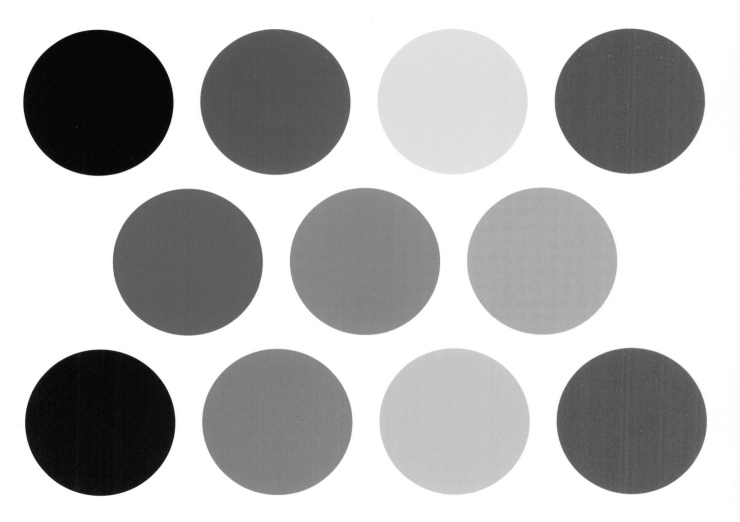

INTRODUCTION

As a Shader Art Director at Pixar for 19 years, it was my job on any given movie to help specify the colors and textures of anything that was modeled for the film. Over the years I've done a lot of thinking about color and the way we use it to help tell our stories.

For me, color acts as the great glue that visually holds everything together. Much like a film soundtrack, it can help shape emotion, provide a smooth transitional arc from one shot to the next, even bind an entire sequence together. Color can direct the eye or move attention away; it can push tension or evoke a sense of tranquility.

Here at Pixar, every film uses a color script to visually map the emotional highs and lows of the story from beginning to end. If the color in the film is working well it can send signals to the audience about the feelings of a scene without one line of dialogue.

The idea for this book—taking single frames from the studio's films and looking at them out of context, using the spectrum of color as a connecting theme—is an unusual one, since these frames are meant to blend seamlessly with one another to create moving images, not static tableaus. Would single images still hold up, I wondered?

After almost 20 years of looking at the studio's films with hyper-attentive eyes, I was not expecting to be as surprised by this book as I was. There were so many startlingly harmonious juxtapositions—"unexpected collisions," we came to call them. I'd see similarities in composition, repetition of shape, and of course, similarity in color. Seeing these individual images would often bring back emotional reminders of what I had felt when first seeing these films, or prompt me to recall minor characters or moments that had been stored away in the deep recesses of my brain. Quite unexpectedly, it helped me see films I thought I knew like the back of my hand in a new way.

As you go through this book, whether quickly or slowly, I challenge you to take the time to see what subtle visuals arise for you. Whatever they are, sit back, and enjoy a spectrum of great color images.

TIA KRATTER

10   Brave, 2012

12   *Toy Story*, 1995

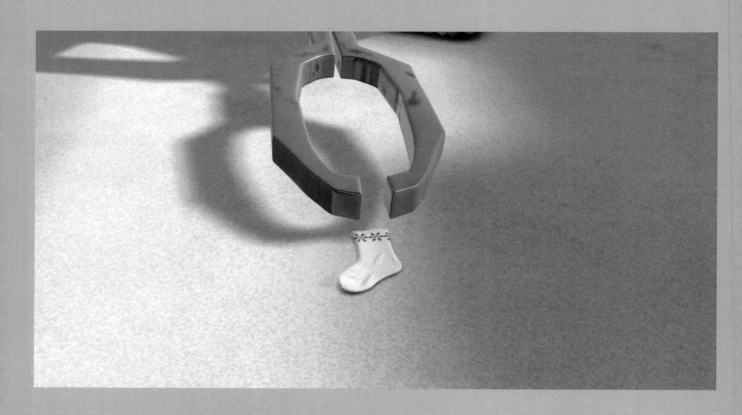

14   *Monsters, Inc.*, 2001

Finding Dory, 2016   15

18   *Finding Dory, 2016*

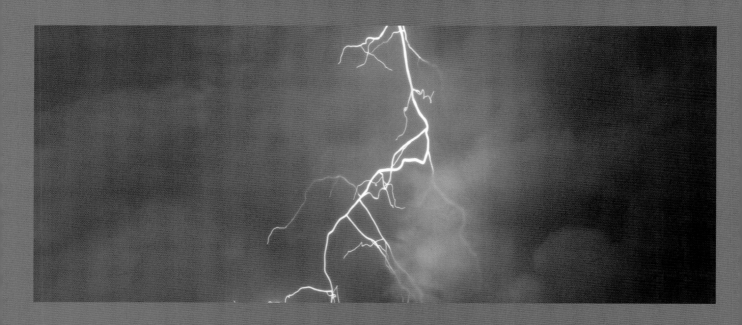

22   *The Good Dinosaur, 2015*

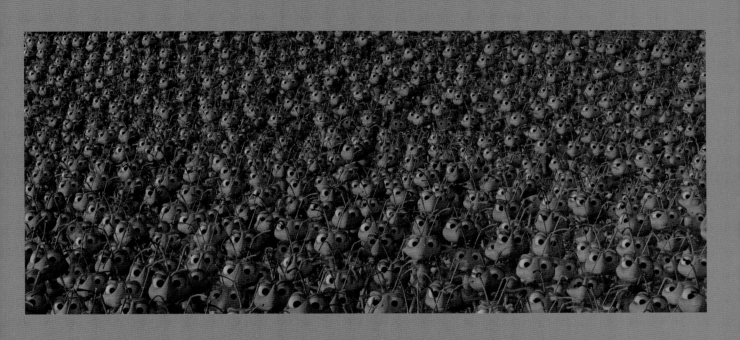

24   A Bug's Life, 1998

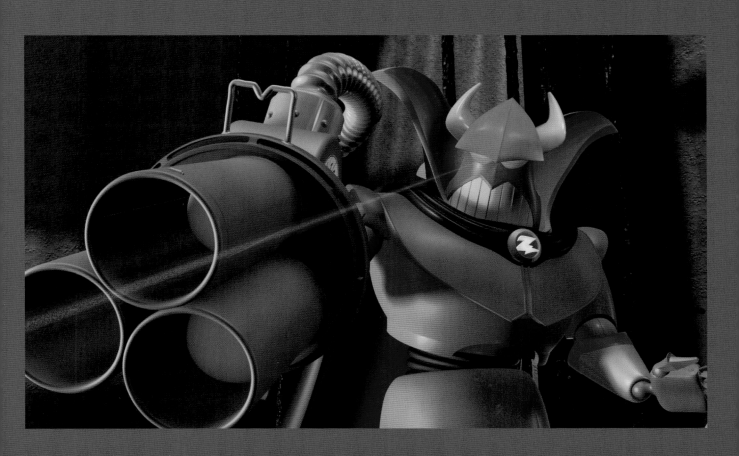

Finding Dory, 2016

34   *Inside Out, 2015*

38   *Inside Out*, 2015

Up, 2009   41

A Bug's Life, 1998

Toy Story 3, 2010   45

Finding Dory, 2016

64   *The Good Dinosaur, 2015*

Monsters, Inc., 2001 67

The Good Dinosaur, 2015

70   *A Bug's Life*, 1998

Finding Dory, 2016

Monsters, Inc., 2001

78   *Finding Nemo*, 2003

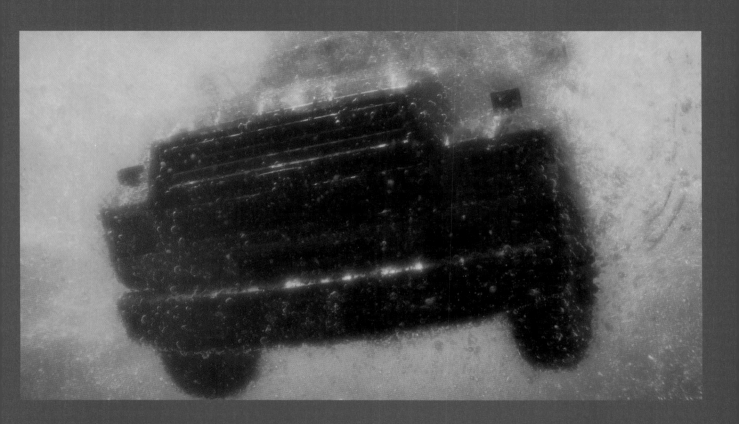

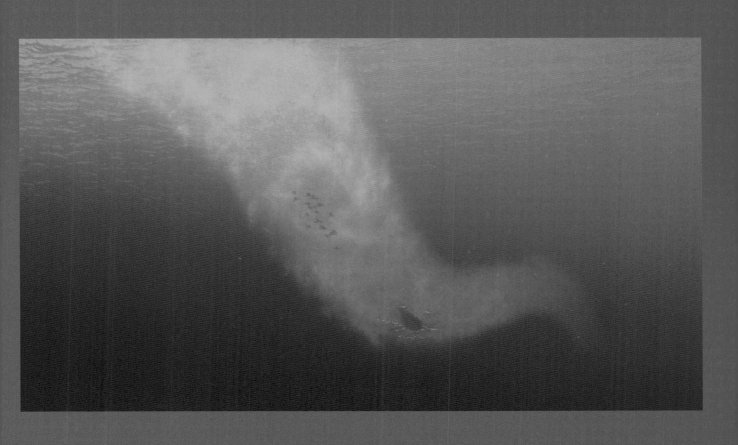

Up, 2009

Monsters, Inc., 2001   91

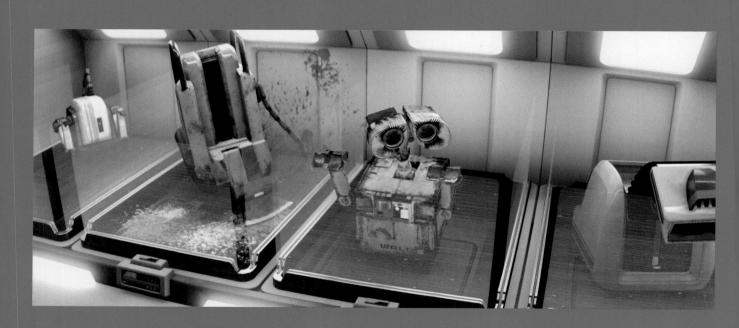

Finding Nemo, 2003

Finding Nemo, 2003

Finding Nemo, 2003

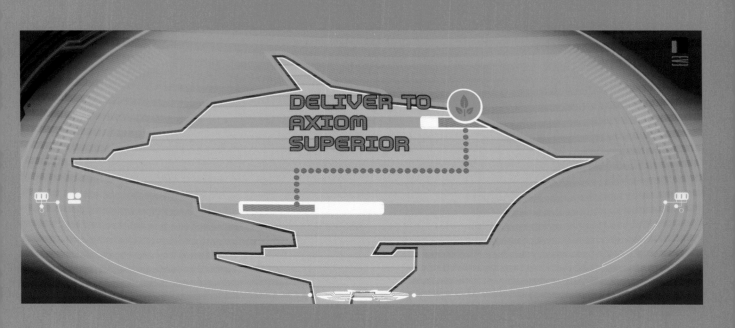

DELIVER TO
AXIOM
SUPERIOR

Toy Story, 1995

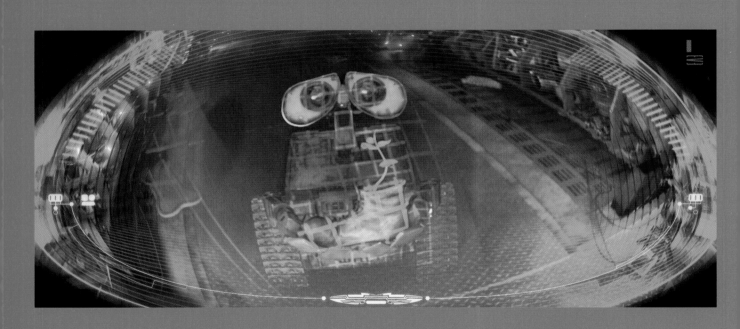

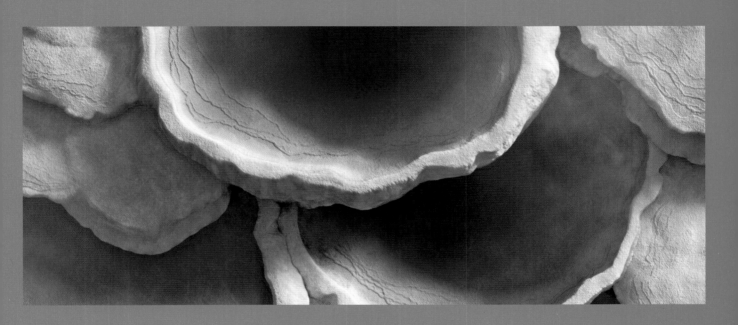

Finding Dory, 2016

The Incredibles, 2004

124   *The Incredibles*, 2004

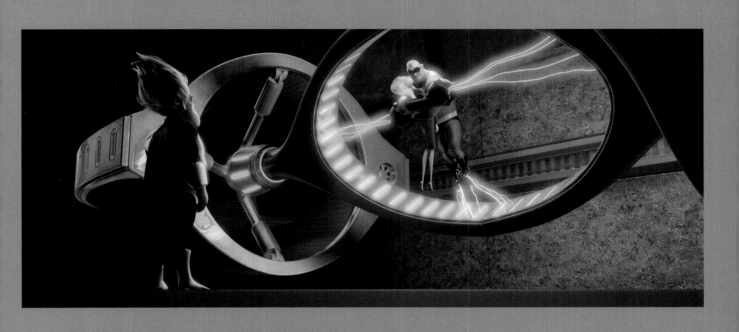

The Incredibles, 2004   129

130   *A Bug's Life*, 1998

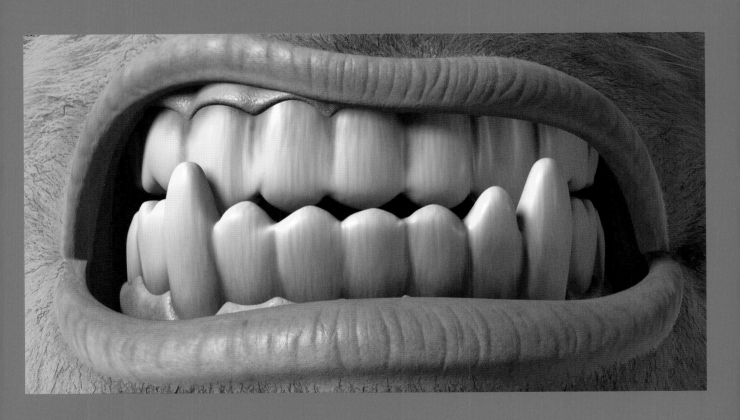

Monsters, Inc., 2001   131

PROJECT KRONOS COUNTDOWN

08 : 10 : 41

HOURS   MINUTES   SECONDS

UNTIL LAUNCH

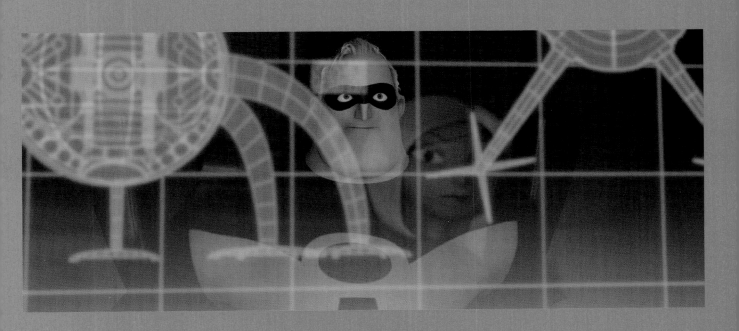

Toy Story, 1995   139

A Bug's Life, 1998   145

148   WALL·E, 2008

The Good Dinosaur, 2015

WALL·E, 2008   151

152　*The Incredibles*, 2004

156   Toy Story 2, 1999

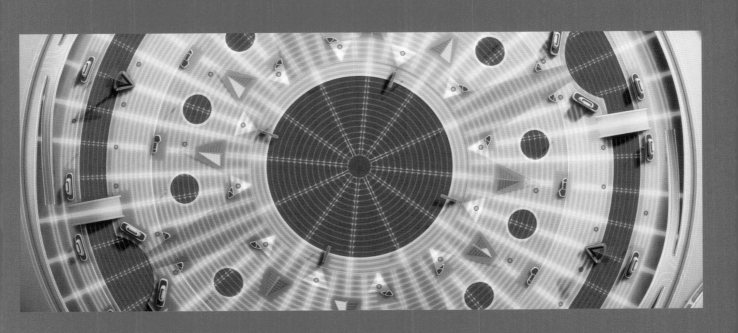

160   *The Good Dinosaur, 2015*

162   A Bug's Life, 1998

164   Up, 2009

166   *Ratatouille, 2007*

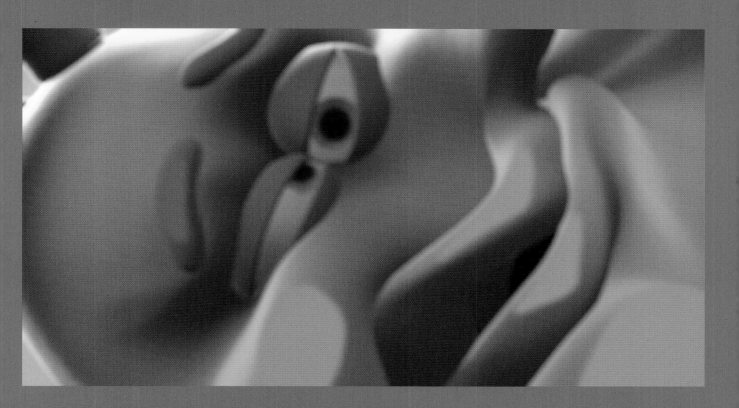

Finding Nemo, 2003   173

176   *Up*, 2009

178   *Finding Dory, 2016*

180   *Finding Nemo*, 2003

182   Toy Story 3, 2010

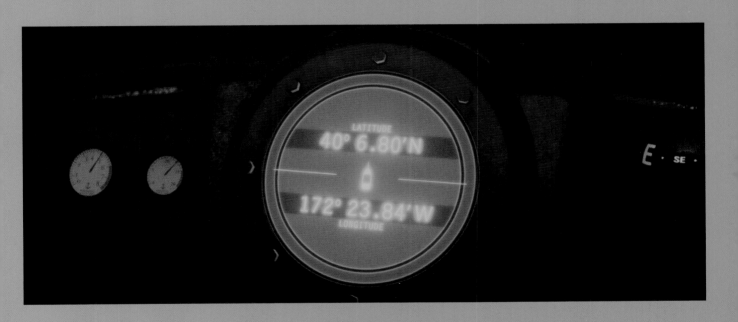

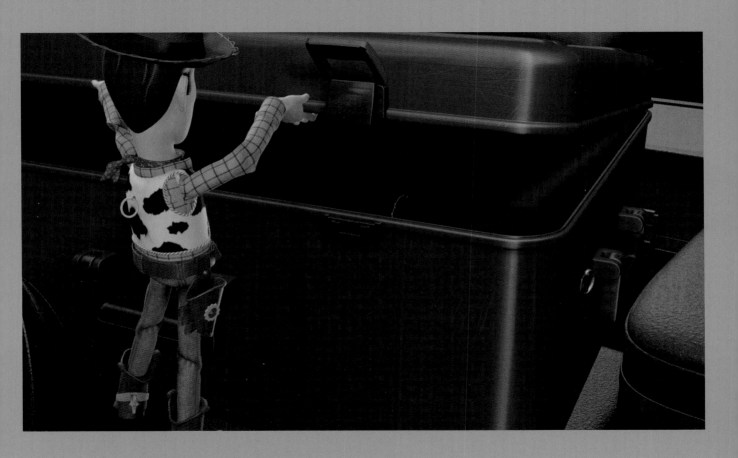

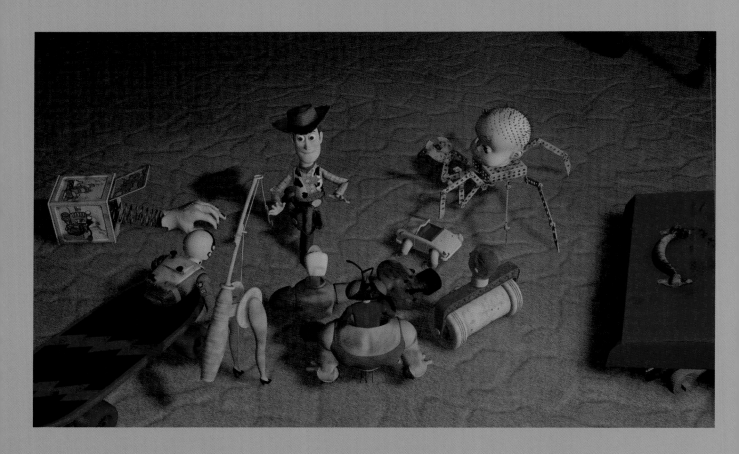

186   *Toy Story.* 1995

188   Toy Story 3, 2010

190   Brave, 2012

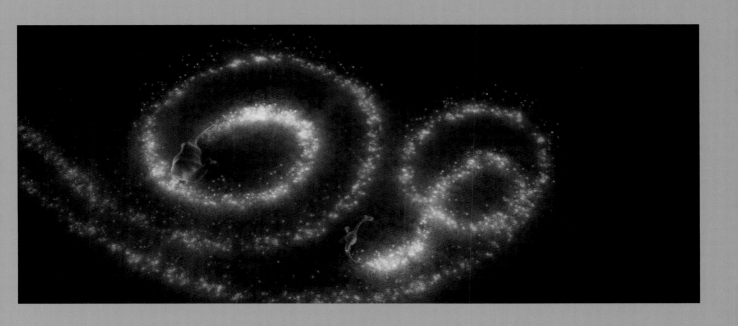

194   *A Bug's Life*, 1998

A Bug's Life, 1998

200   *Inside Out, 2015*

Up, 2009   201

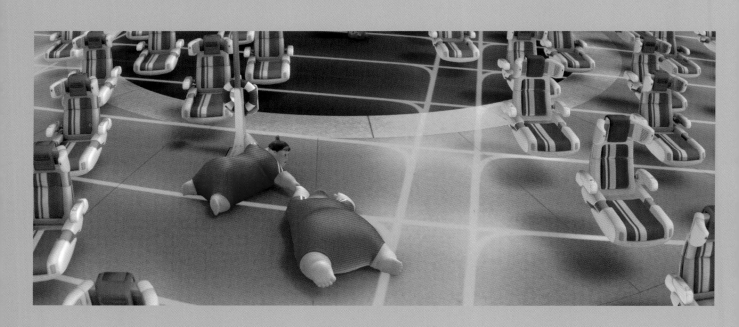

208   A Bug's Life, 1998

210   Toy Story 2, 1999

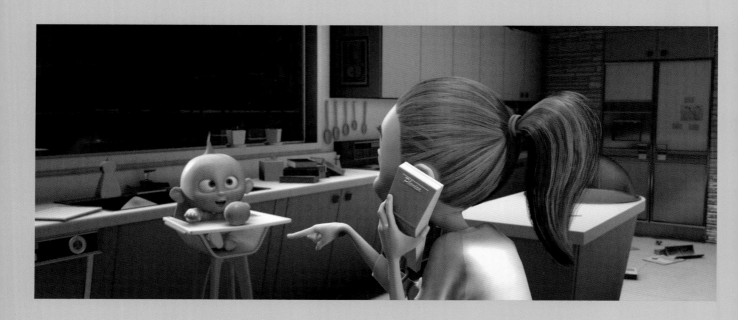

The Incredibles, 2004

214   *A Bug's Life*, 1998

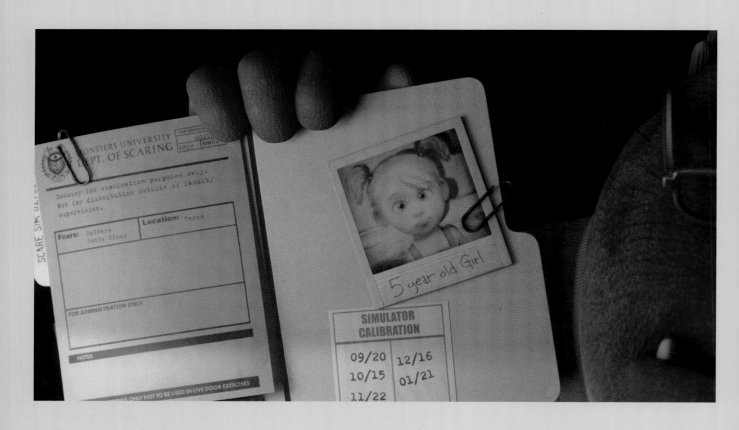

222   *A Bug's Life*, 1998

224   A Bug's Life, 1998

226 Toy Story 3, 2010

228 WALL·E, 2008

232   Up, 2009

234   WALL·E, 2008

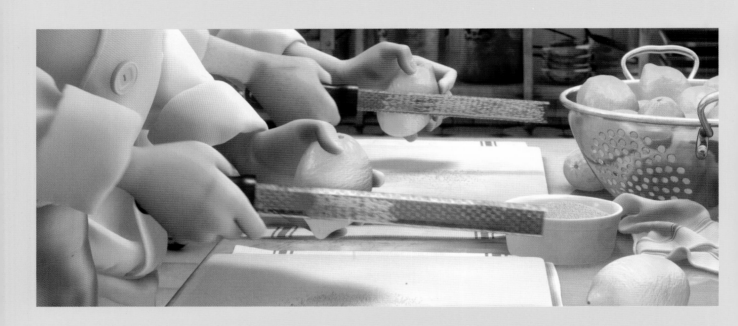

236　Ratatouille, 2007

240   Ratatouille, 2007

Toy Story 2, 1999   241

244   Toy Story 2, 1999

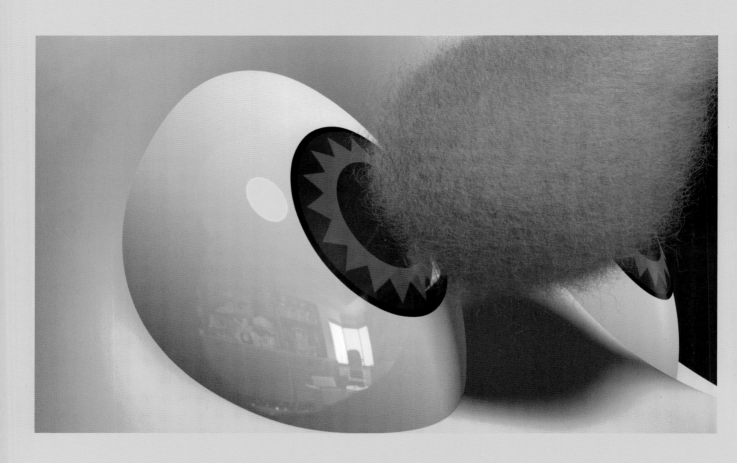

248   Toy Story 2, 1999

252   WALL·E, 2008

Brave, 2012   253

254   *A Bug's Life*, 1998

256　Toy Story 3, 2010

260 *The Good Dinosaur*, 2015

264   Inside Out, 2015

268   *The Incredibles*, 2004

Toy Story 2, 1999   269

272   *The Incredibles*, 2004

CHICK'S PICKS
CHICK HICKS
FORMER AND FOREVER
PISTON CUP
CHAMPION
PISTON CUP
86
RSN
CHICK HICKS

FRIGHTON ELEMENTARY SCHOOL

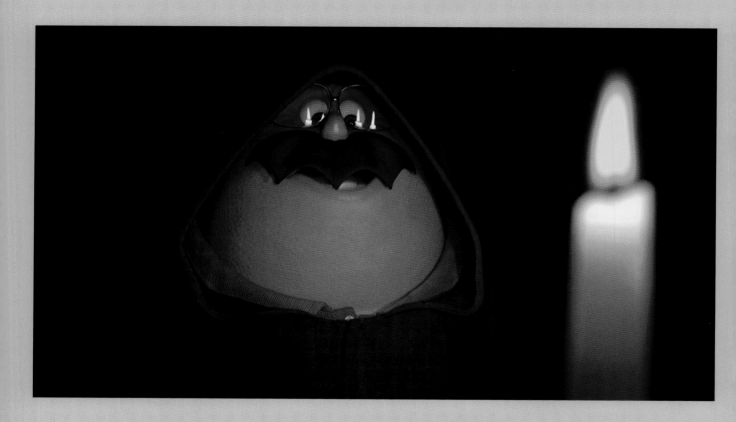

282   *The Good Dinosaur*, 2015

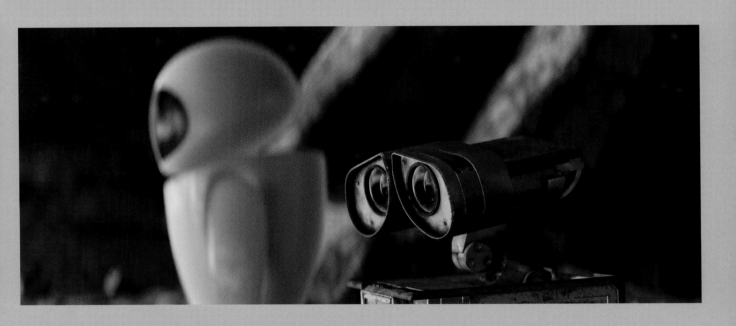

WALL·E, 2008   283

284   *The Incredibles*, 2004

OUT FOR SEASON

Hudson Hornet does a cartwheel into the infield after hitting the outside wall. Champ was hurt badly in crash.

286   Cars, 2006

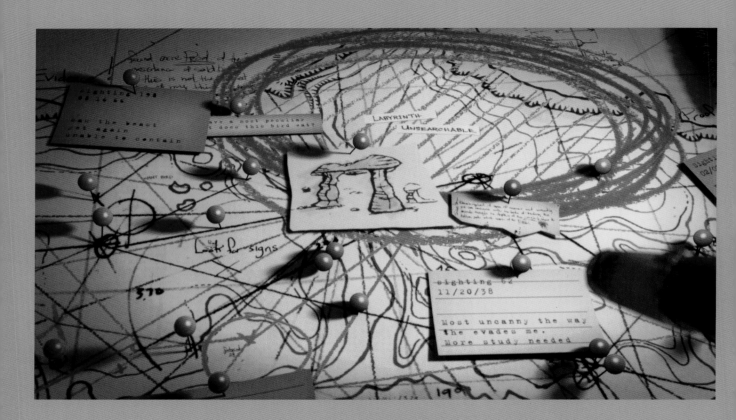

Ratatouille, 2007

292 Cars, 2006

294   *The Incredibles, 2004*

Finding Nemo, 2003   295

Cars 2, 2011

CPT CHG SRV

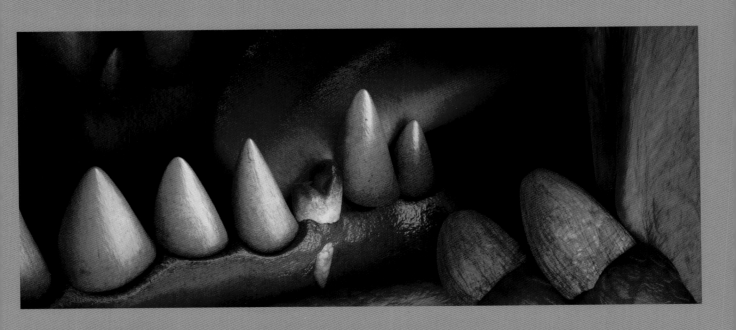

302 *Toy Story, 1995*

Up, 2009   303

304   *Up, 2009*

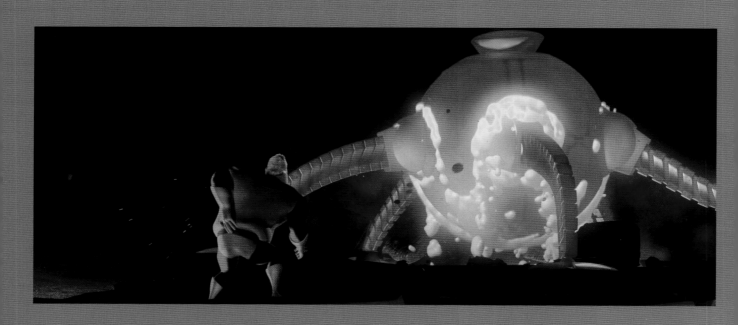

306   *The Incredibles*, 2004

312   WALL·E, 2008

314   Finding Dory, 2016

316   *Up*, 2009

318   *Toy Story*, 1995

320   *Brave*, 2012

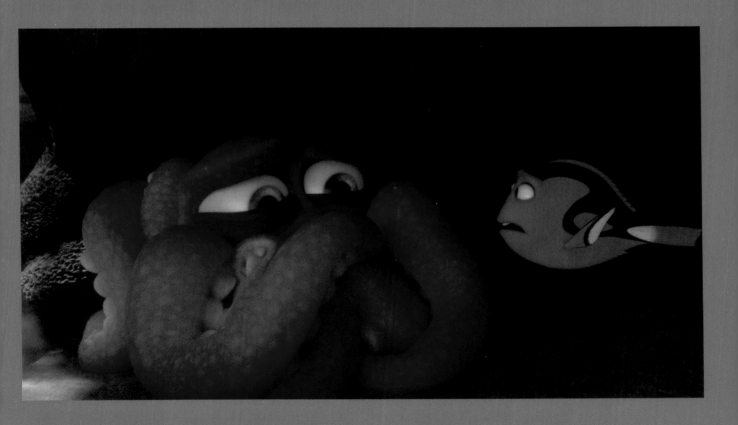

322   *Ratatouille, 2007*

324 *Finding Nemo*, 2003

326   Monsters University, 2013

Monsters, Inc., 2001   329

330　*The Incredibles, 2004*

332 Monsters University, 2013

334   *Inside Out, 2015*

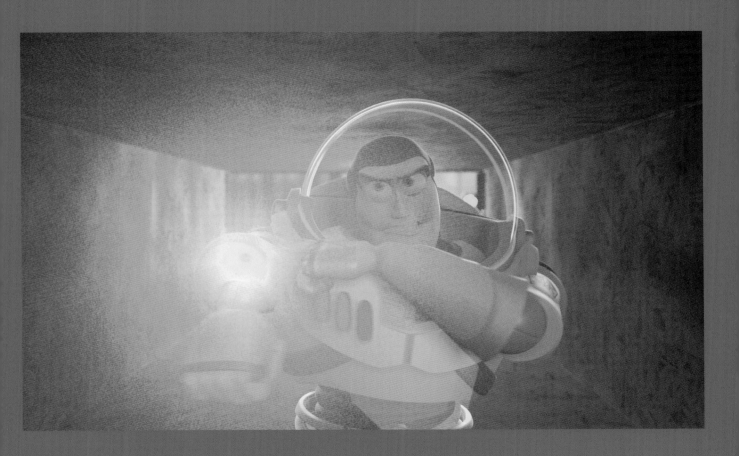

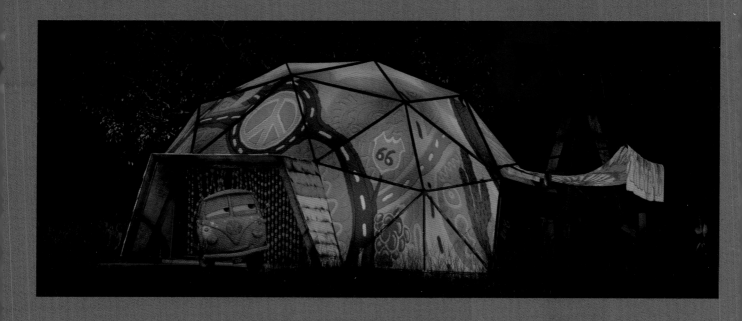

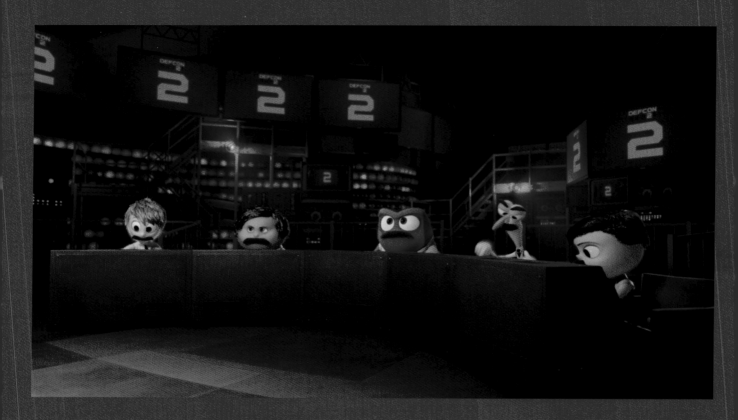

338 *Inside Out*, 2015

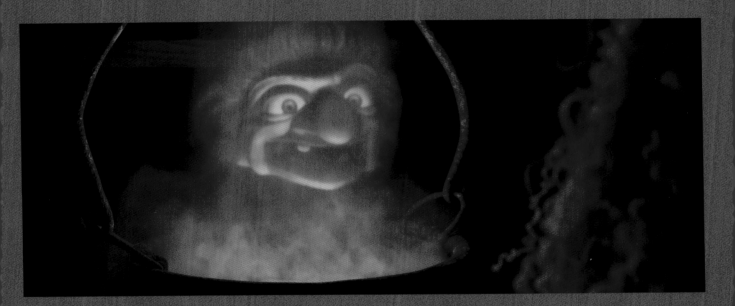

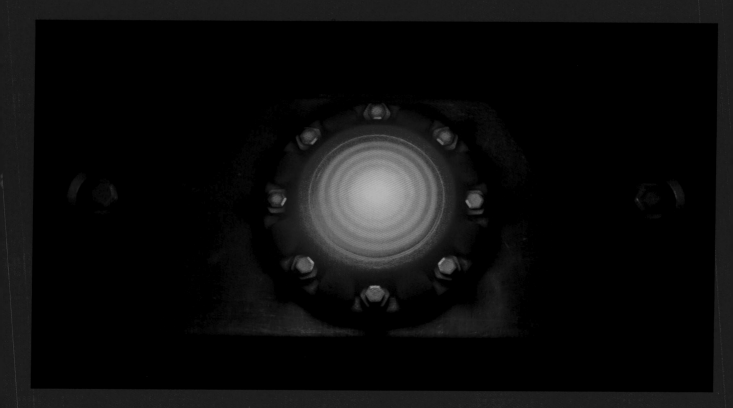

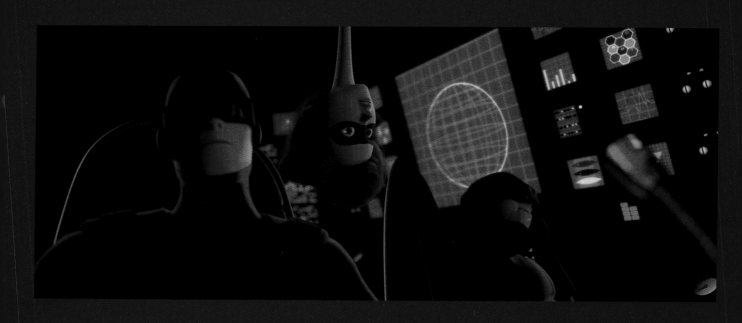

342　*The Incredibles*, 2004

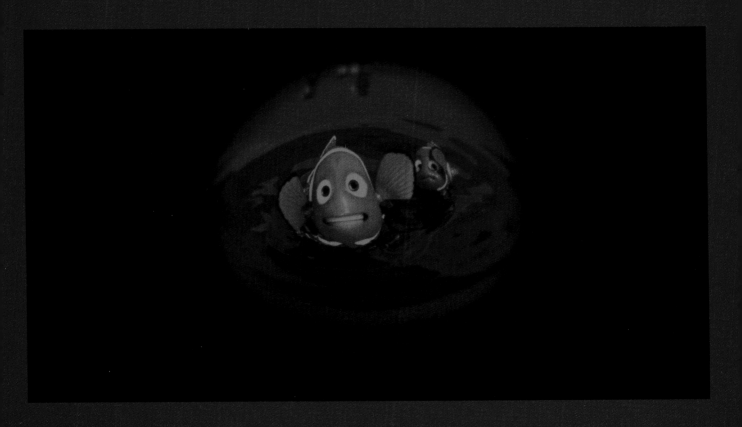

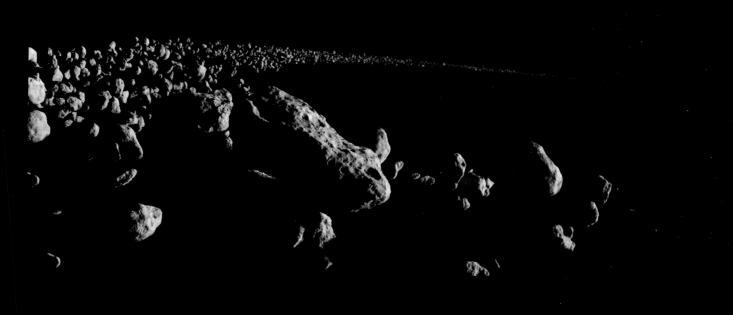

346   Brave, 2012

348   *Inside Out, 2015*

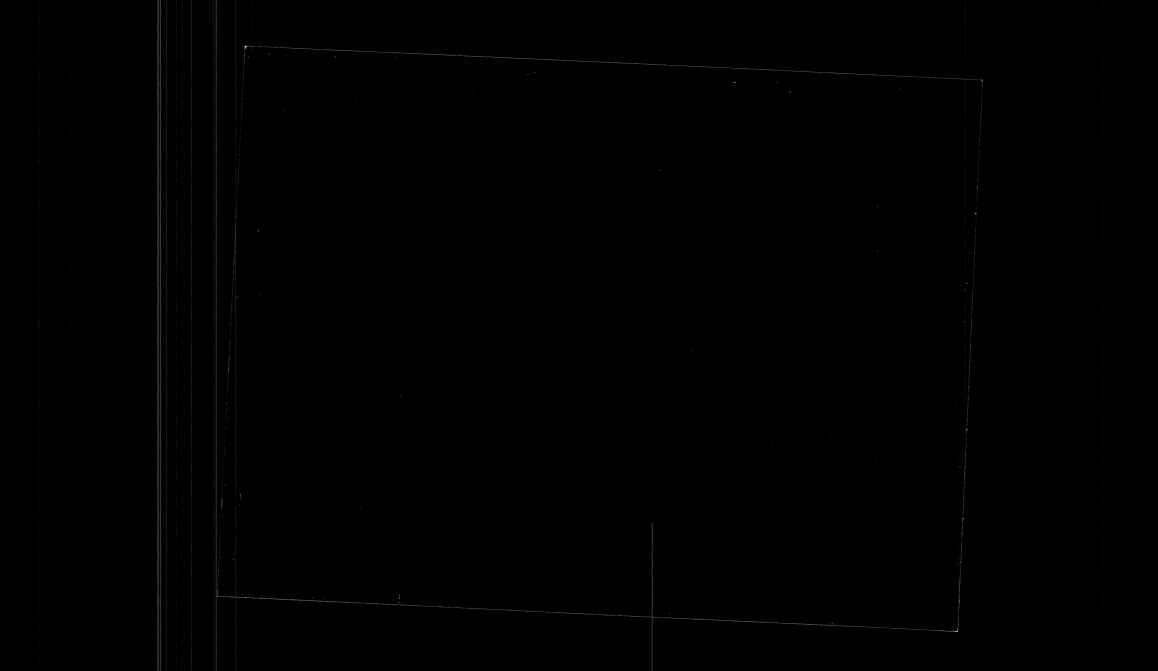

ACKNOWLEDGMENTS

My heartfelt thanks . . .

To Neil, Wynn, Beth, and Lia at Chronicle Books for being so lovely and positive to work with, and to designer Liam for his keen eye (can we do it again?).

To Jenny for your smiling enthusiasm, and to Molly for keeping us on track. To Clay Welch and Cynthia Lusk for rendering the images we requested, and to Karen Paik for making me sound better than I really do.

To everyone at Pixar who touched one of these films, thank you for making beautiful images for me to pair together.

To Pauly, Joel and Marshall for treating me like one of the guys, and to Dre, for letting me be a girl.

To Biggie, who let me play with art while growing up.

To JL, who allowed me to play with color and texture as an adult. What a ride it's been.

Library of Congress Cataloging-in-Publication
Data is available.

ISBN: 978-1-4521-5920-1

Manufactured in China

Cover and book design by **Neil Egan**
Layout and composition by **Liam Flanagan**

10 9 8 7 6 5 4 3 2 1

Chronicle Books LLC
680 Second Street
San Francisco, CA 94107
www.chroniclebooks.com